LOOK UP

A GUIDE FOR NAVIGATING LIFE'S UNCERTAINTIES & FINDING YOUR HORIZON

RACHEL HAVEKOST

**THOUGHT
CATALOG**
Books

THOUGHTCATALOG.COM

Published by Thought Catalog Books, an imprint of Thought Catalog, a digital magazine owned and operated by The Thought & Expression Co. Inc., an independent media organization founded in 2010 and based in the United States of America. For stocking inquiries, contact stockists@shopcatalog.com.

Produced by Chris Lavergne and Noelle Beams
Art direction and design by KJ Parish
Circulation management by Isidoros Karamitopoulos

thoughtcatalog.com | shopcatalog.com

First Limited Edition Print
Printed in the United States of America, SHD 2025

ISBN 978-1-965820-09-4

LO
OK
UP

A collection of poems and short love
notes: encouragement for times of wild
uncertainty, loving reminders for recovery
and change, and ultimately, small moments
of great comfort: *this is not who you are,
this is something you are going through.*

Reminders, to look up.

"Look Up" is dedicated to all the girl's girls—especially mine.

A PROLOGUE OF SORTS

You will have seasons of life when you'll wonder if anything will ever work out. You'll doubt yourself or feel stuck. You'll question if it's worth trying to get up again when you're just going to fall once more. You'll feel seasons of hope and recovery and forget the painful ones. You'll lose sight of how much you've grown, and when the stuckness comes again, you'll feel defeated. These seasons will come and go, rise and fall, and just like you, they'll persist.

I find myself in this cycle often. Despite decades of therapy, research, and spiritual study, I return to a state of overwhelming loss. These periods can lead me to feeling hopeless and disgruntled, as if I've failed myself by coming back.

At times these cycles have kept me stuck long enough to wonder, *will I ever emerge, or will I always find myself back here?*

I remember (as I do every time I'm in this season of stuckness) that even though it feels like nothing is happening or coming together, and even though I have no idea what direction I'm going or how to get there, that one day I'll look back on this time and say, "oh yeah, it was all working out, I just couldn't see how then because I was in it."

The truth is, we will all find ourselves back here: in the doubt, in the stuck, in the loss. It is life's natural balance: life and death, love and loss, pleasure and pain...to know one is to know the other, and it would be foolish to chase a life absent of any discomfort. Still, these seasons of pain have the ability to break us. Without the right support, tools, or compassion, our pain becomes suffering and we become *truly* stuck.

I hope this book finds you when you're stuck. I hope this book finds you when you're afraid. I hope this book finds you when you're doubting that good things will come or when you're seeped in grief or on the precipice of change. I hope this book can serve as the companion you may not have right now. The compassion you may not have access to. Wisdom you may feel too clouded to see, or the tools you may feel too tired to reach for. I hope this book finds you when you're ready to shift in the cycle and move forward in life.

When you're ready to *Look Up*.

A MAP TO THIS BOOK

Look Up is divided into seven sections: *Holding On; Opening the Heart; Roaming Free; Integrating; Zooming Out; Opening the Mind; & Navigating Forward.*

Think of this book as a map of sorts: a tender guide for moving through life's big questions, love lost, and hearts found. This guide is not meant to be a how-to or what-to-do: rather a hand to hold while you forge your own path.

I invite you to read from beginning to end, especially if you are finding this book in a time of grief, uncertainty, or change.

Of course, this is your book, your life, and your time, so if you want to flip through the pages and land somewhere in the middle and start there, please do.

You'll find what you need no matter where you start, for the truth is we are always at the beginning, constantly at the end, and forever right here, in the middle.

There is no right way, there is the only way you do it.

HOLDING ON

read this when you feel like you can't let go. when you feel stuck or trapped or unable to see what's next. when all you want is to go back in time, when the future looks hazy, when it's easier to feel pain in the familiar than find peace in the unknown. read this when it's time to begin again.

/the end/

when you find yourself at the beginning of things: new relationships or newly single, a new job or the start of another school year, moving in with friends and new kitchen tile, the first chapter, the first episode, the first run in new sneakers, setting boundaries and practicing coping skills, saying "yes" to the scary thing and "no" to the scarier thing, a new album by your favorite band and the first song of a summer concert, the first steps after surgery and finally trying your hand at painting. when you find yourself at the beginning of things you'll feel stuck and scared and unready. when you find yourself at the beginning of things you'll wonder if you're capable of navigating the newness and you'll doubt yourself. when you find yourself at the beginning of things you'll forget that everything you've ever done, *you once did as a beginner*: the first time you brushed your own hair and wrote your own name, the first time you said "hi" to a crush and raised your hand in class, the first time you spoke up for yourself or made yourself dinner, the first time you picked up your prescription or went to a bar, the first time you took the bus and cried alone and cleaned up someone else's mess and the first time you said "i'm sorry." when you find yourself at the beginning of things *and you know it's the beginning*, remember your body has begun countless times without you ever realizing it. you know how to begin. you always have. when you find yourself at the beginning of things, hold yourself tenderly and remind yourself that *you can do new things.* close your eyes and remember that while uncertainty is scary for the human mind, it is also an opportunity to create anything you can imagine. then, look up.

some days you won't have the strength to swim. *look up.* you'll float and wonder if the ocean is even real—if perhaps you've already drowned and this is some kind of afterlife. *look up.* you'll feel a rage boil and start to kick and scream. you'll want someone to hear your heartbreak but your voice will be muffled and lost in the wind and sea. you'll want the memories to disappear; maybe an empty mind will make you lighter. you'll ask a thousand questions but the answers won't come. *look up.* the swim will test you, and you'll feel alone. the swim will exhaust you, and you'll feel doubt. but the swim will not kill you, and you will make it to land. *look up.*

/and then one day/

i wasn't me anymore
and the life i thought i'd have
washed away with the sea
no matter how thick i laid the sand
around my cold wet body
the ocean always came to wash it away.

sometimes you won't be ready to
hear the light is coming. sometimes
you'll just need someone to sit in
the darkness with you until it does.

you're allowed to long for good things even if you believe you don't deserve them yet. sometimes it's in this longing that we teach ourselves to believe we're worth something more.

one day you'll look down and see the sand between your toes, wet and sticky. you'll pull one foot out, then the other. *maybe i can bring some with me,* you'll think hopefully. shoving the wet sand in your pockets like keepsakes; treasures that lost their shape but surely could shine again; dissolving between the fabric of your jeans—you'll lose it—the sand, and them. you'll want to scoop them up. you'll want to try again, to take the sand with you. you'll cry a little, wonder if the salt on your face is your own or the sea's. you'll stare at your feet and watch them sink and want to become the sand itself. you'll realize the sand will never mold to what you want it to be, and you're going to let it go. you'll pull one foot out, then the other. *i cannot bring it with me,* you'll think knowingly. you'll take one, big breath through your nose, smell the salty air and all the sea, let out one last cry, and sigh, *i'm ready now.*

we are afraid to let go because we
don't want to forget. you can let go
and still remember what you've lost.

some days you'll wonder where you'll get the energy. on those days you'll tell yourself, *just this moment, just this task.* you'll focus on just the next right thing. when your mind says *i can't* or *how will i?* you'll notice, and with a gentle pause reply, *one step at a time.*

your grief is a only a reflection of how much you loved. truly experiencing grief means you truly loved.

you are not your grief or your doubt or your hope. you are experiencing all of them, *yes*. they exist and are real, *yes*. and they are not *you*. they do not become or consume you and you cannot become or consume them. when you can separate yourself from your feelings and your experiences, you can center yourself in a state of non-attachment; this doesn't mean a state of complacency or *de*tachment, it means a willingness to stay connected to what you're feeling without cutting off your emotional world—interested in others without enmeshing—curious, observant, and present. the challenge is to let your feelings exist and walk beside them without abandoning them. hold their hand and ask them questions. stay *you*, and stay *with* them. watch your thoughts float by and notice them. acknowledge the urge to swim with them or hold them upstream. *stay you*. what you are feeling or holding or processing is not you—it is a strong current you are swimming through, a harsh wind gusting beside you, or a cold snow that soon will pass. greet your grief as a visitor, and it will teach you to honor the storm without becoming it.

this is not who you are.
this is something you're going through.

look up.

OPENING THE HEART

read this when you know it's time to move on. even if it hurts. even if you still love what's lost. even if you're not ready. read this when you're letting go.

you can sit at the water's edge
admiring the horizon all you like
but the only way you'll know
what life is like on the other side
is to get in the water
and swim.

you cannot swim across the ocean in just one stroke. nor could you make the journey overnight. there might be storms or harsh cold winds. you'll need to rest. you'll need to wait. you'll need to float for days on end just to see the sky and know it's all just one great adventure. and in the end, when you do find land, you'll look back on the sea you swam across and know how much you would have missed if all it took was a single stroke.

one day you'll look back on this time of your life with awe and say, "that was the part where i sat with my pain. that was the part where i stopped kicking. that was the part where i had the courage to feel it all. that was the part where i finally let go."

the courage to let go is also the courage to begin again. the courage to start over is also the courage to end a chapter. when you have the strength to do one, you undoubtedly have the strength to do the other.

when the end is not in sight or you're too tired to go on, you have not failed. you've simply been swimming across the vast and open sea and your body needs rest from the paddling.

"she's floating by,"
they'll say cunningly.

"no,"
you'll sternly reply.

"i'm finally letting go."

letting go will hurt,
but it won't kill you.
you'll live to tell the story
of how you got your scars,
and how you survived.

/and then one day/

i felt rocks beneath my toes
arms outstretched
i felt my belly press against salty seaweed
clutching solid ground
floating towards the land
no longer surrounded by endless
and directionless water
i had arrived
but where, i couldn't say
i had arrived
but i was lost
there on all fours
with new sand between my fingers
cold water washed the seaweed from my skin
standing, limbs quivering,
my still two feet
on ground i didn't recognize
in a tired, beaten body
i had arrived
but all i wanted to do
was go home.

there will be moments when you look back across the sea you've crossed and wonder what it might be like to go back. wonder who might still be there and if they'd still want you. wonder if by the time you returned you'd even recognize each other. wonder if you could have the chance to try again, to make it right, to change the outcome. this wondering will haunt you if you give it too much air, rob you of the chance to grow if you stuff it too far down, and return again if you do not let it go. let yourself look back on where you came from and wonder how all that's passed has shaped you, what choices you'll make to build roots on new soil, and why you left in the first place.

the truth is that nothing new happens in the past. it's normal to want to hold on to it, even if it wasn't good for you, even if it was hurting you, even if it was already dead. but no amount of holding on will bring something back to life. sometimes, all we can do is plant new seeds and try to grow something new again.

the truth is also that we attach to the past because it's familiar. our brains love *familiarity* because knowing is *safe*. knowing is *predictable*. predictable is *security*, even if the predictable is *killing us*. the truth is also that there are so many people, memories, places, and versions of yourself waiting for you in the unfamiliar, unpredictable, and great unknown.

just because it's familiar
doesn't mean it's safe.

ROAMING FREE

read this when you feel lost in life. when nothing is certain and all that's familiar is behind you. read this when you feel aimless and without direction, naked and exposed, raw and unhinged. read this when you've finally let go.

if you can muster up the will to leave spaces that haunt you, you can muster up the will to enter spaces that scare you. if your heart has the strength to let go, it has the strength to begin again. the hard part isn't loosening your grip nor clutching anew—it's sitting empty-handed in the space between that hurts the most.

it is dark and quiet here
in the nothingness
i do not know which way to go
so sometimes i lay my head on the
ground and just look up
i ask the stars for signs
i ask the moon for light
i ask someone, somewhere, to show me where to go
for surely this lost land
has a map for me to follow
surely i am not meant to make a home alone
surely there is some right way to make it all ok again
i fall asleep
cold sandy air cakes my skin at first morning light
and still
it's just me
oh, *it's just me.*

/and then one day/

i realized no one would make
my new life for me
and worse, if i let them,
it wouldn't be mine at all
and i'd lose myself all over again
"put on your coat,"
i say to myself.
"we're going out to find ourselves now."

open spaces scare you because it's in this vastness that all directions are possible, and you're forced to face the limitlessness of your potential. imagine what could happen if you let yourself find out.

life after loss or change or rupture are not waiting times or limbo states—they are places you go to find yourself again. places you go to find each other again. places you go to find hope and courage and believe in life beyond what you once knew. life after anything is just more life.

you will feel lost in life. you'll say you don't know what you want. that you don't know who you are. you'll say this with some veil of shame—as if it's a bad thing. but most people are lost. most people have no idea what they're doing. for the most part, people are making it up as they go. as soon as you think you have a grip on life it will change in ways you could never have predicted. the older you get, the more you'll realize it's fruitless to hold on to what you think life should be or how it will go, because you'll know this only leads to disappointment or feeling like a failure. you'll stop berating yourself for feeling lost and cherish your outlook for choosing curiosity. you'll try new things, *again*, and wonder what this life thing is all about. you'll have deep chats at bars and read philosophy in parks. you'll feel more comfortable with your life. you'll say you know what you want and that you finally know who you are. you'll say this with some veil of hope—as if nothing is bad or good, as if you've finally realized that "lost" is not a place to run from, but the place between what's known and unknown. that being lost is a sign that you were brave, and you're on your way to something new.

life going differently than you planned is not bad. it doesn't mean you failed or did something wrong. it means you were brave and you tried. it means you were honest with yourself when something wasn't working. it means you're allowing yourself to take up the space in the life that you want, instead of wasting time in a life that you don't.

you're lost between
then
and
now
but doesn't
between
still mean
you're *somewhere*?

maybe you're not lost. maybe you're finding new perspectives. rearranging things to find a better place for them. making mistakes so you can learn from them in the future. planting new seeds to find out what you can grow. maybe you're trying new things so you can learn what you like and what you don't like. maybe you're seeing life with a childlike wonder and curiosity. maybe you're figuring out what life means to *you* and carving your *own* path. maybe you're not lost. maybe you're exploring.

when the voice in your head says, *you're going to do it wrong,* i hope you reply with courage, *but what if i don't do it at all?*

when you're starting to find yourself, you'll spend a lot of time alone. in these times, you'll face the parts of yourself that haven't been nourished. you'll feel empty and long for something to make that feeling go away, so much that you might betray yourself in the pursuit of it. say yes to things you don't want to do in hopes that it might fill the void. backpedal on boundaries thinking it might open up opportunities to connect and ease the loneliness. abandon yourself thinking that if you were just *good* enough, you might finally feel relief. but every time you cross your own boundaries or leave yourself, you break your own trust. and the more you break your own trust, the lonelier you'll feel. if you want to ease the loneliness, you'll have to stop abandoning yourself and start showing up. you'll have to stick to your boundaries and honor your needs. you'll have to be true to what you want and firmly stand in your own skin. you'll have to act in line with what you believe and be unwaveringly comfortable with your desires. you'll have to see your loneliness not as a hole to fill but as a wound to heal.

empty times call for filling
feeding with new flavors and
answering with new ideas
when all is lost
and you've let go of so much
the body will feel restless for the filling
do nourish
do refuel
do experiment
remember the body will get sick from the newness
and these rejections are not signs of failure
but redirection
you will listen and reroute
you will hear them and have patience
you will continue to fill the emptiness with *you*
until the body is ripe with color
and full
and *you*.

when life feels unbearable and the only out feels like ending it all, when you're screaming and crying in your hands to muffle the sound shouting, "i want a do over!" ask yourself, "what would i do if i could start from scratch? what would i do differently?" and do that.

INTEGRATING

read this when you're starting to know yourself. when you're learning what it means to be free. when you're bound to no one but you, and for the first time in your life, you like what you see in the mirror. read this when you've met the version of yourself you always knew existed, even if it's scary, even if it's foreign, even if it's painful. read this when you're becoming you.

every magnificent painting
was once a blank canvas.

/and then one day/

i made myself a home.
a small but cozy place to call my own.
walls with art i made
or found
mismatched chairs and a
window for watching the sea
and the place my garden might grow
a few utensils
enough for guests
(should i make a friend)
and one orange;
something to last
peel with lovers
or watch rot
these floors might be crooked
but they are mine.

i once picked flowers from my mother's garden. i looked at her in awe and asked how she grew them. she said, "it's never too late to start something new. i didn't know what i was doing when i started. i still don't, i just have more confidence now. that's the difference."

for the first time in a long time
the soil is mine and mine alone
roses?
no.
tulips?
perhaps.
a small gazebo for moonlit music
patches of grass for endless dancing
yes.
this garden of mine is mine to grow
how utterly terrifying
and wildly free.

if you plant roses
because someone told you
they loved their petals,
don't forget
it will always be your job
to trim the thorns
whether you love roses too,
or not.

little bugs and birds have
wandered into my little life
i name them, one by one
they become my friends
the bugs and birds.
it's too scary still to know what
you might think of me
so until i know what i think of myself
i'll let the sound of bugs and birds
softly fill the silence.

don't rob yourself the opportunity of
becoming a butterfly, simply because all
you've ever known is being a caterpillar.

how will i know when i'm truly me?
when is it safe to venture back out—
out there in the unknown?
my garden has become so lush
i'm afraid to leave it
what if it dies while i'm away?
should someone destroy or terrorize it?
what if i forget it altogether,
become consumed by all that's out *there*?
peering beyond the flowers and
brush i've built myself,
i shed a tiny tear.
i hold myself and inhale the sweetness i've created
close my eyes and whisper,
"you will not forget her.
you will not abandon her.
she will not be disturbed,
and you will come back each day to water her.
she is not something you made to leave and lose.
she is your soil, she is your home,
she is you."

you will lose a lot of things in your life. you'll lose people / places / jobs / lovers / friends / memories / identities / masks you once wore /material goods / money / musical tastes / taste buds / your hearing / favorite bars / baristas / inspiration / souvenirs...you will lose a lot in your life, but the one thing i hope you never lose is you.

you might not be something for everyone, but you will be everything for someone.

you can stand upon the bridge and ask which way to go but the bridge will never tell you. you can sit below the bridge for shelter but when it's time to leave, the bridge will not go with you. you can clutch the ledge of the bridge's edge, wonder what the fall might feel like, but the bridge will never catch you. it is only when you cross the bridge and walk away, that you know the bridge is you.

sometimes healing is less about altering what isn't working and more about adding what's missing. saying yes to experiences with new people. trying on different personalities or hobbies. being open to life as a beginner and making big mistakes. remembering over and over that feeling anxiety or sorrow or loneliness doesn't make you sick, it makes you human.

i think feeling lonely is actually quite a beautiful thing—our emotions are there to communicate something, and loneliness tells us we need to seek connection. connection is how we survive, so loneliness, in many ways, is a reminder of how much we truly want to live.

the hardest thing you'll do in life is say goodbye. goodbye to people, goodbye to places, goodbye to parts of yourself. don't forget that with every goodbye comes a "hello," and it's only when you turn away from all you've said farewell to that you'll see how many hellos are waiting to greet you.

hello.

ZOOMING OUT

read this when you're branching back out. when you've healed or recovered or done the work and you're ready to test your new wings. read this when you've discovered more of who you are and what you want, and when it's time to venture out into the world and find it.

/and then one day/

i left my home to meet the world
risked my orange rotting
in the kitchen window
knowing i'd rather lick
someone else's sticky fingers
than eat oranges
alone.

you know what happens when you stop fearing rejection? you get rejected. over and over and over. but then, something else happens. you meet people who love you so deeply that you can't imagine ever pretending to be someone you're not ever again.

find more people who remind you what life is really about. surround yourself with them. bask in the nourishment that is true connection beyond the physical. beyond the material. beyond the counting or quantifying and into the childlike wonder and delight in living.

this might be hard to believe, but when people love you, they think you deserve the world. once you start to understand this, you'll realize the hardest part isn't believing that other people want the best for you; it's asking yourself if you think you deserve the world, too. because at the end of the day, one of those people has to be you.

if you show up in a mask and someone loves your mask, then the "real you" underneath is going to be a surprise. but if you show up as you, someone will love *you*, and then there is nothing to hide.

growing up, you'll spend a lot of time trying to fit in. this is normal; as adolescents, our primary focus is assessing ourselves in social spaces. instead of looking up to authority for answers, we look adjacently to our peers. our sense of worth is at risk during these times; without ample opportunity to balance safe boundary-setting and risk-taking, exploration both socially and personally, we may start to attach to the outside world to confirm our value. we wear masks to fit into places we think will enhance our worth. try to prove ourselves to people we think we need approval from. do all we can to be understood in spaces that will never understand us. as adults, this leaves us feeling isolated in social settings, misunderstood in intimate ones, and as if something is simply wrong with us. the truth is, nothing is wrong with you; you're just not being *you*. if you show up as you really are, the people who are meant for you won't need an explanation. you'll be you, and they'll love you for it.

stop trying to get people to like you
and start allowing people to see you.

if you pursue something outside of yourself to ease your loneliness you will always feel empty inside. this kind of loneliness is not about being alone and needing human connection. do that. that is good. this kind of loneliness is about every time you break your own trust by abandoning yourself so that someone might love you or something might soothe you. and every time you break this trust and leave yourself, the loneliness only gets bigger. you'll constantly seek to fill the void with something outside of yourself until you stop self-betraying and start showing up for yourself. the void is not a hole to fill; it's a wound to mend.

learning to stay open to new friendships and new love and new people is messy and triggering and terrifying. and, every so often, you'll meet people who are willing to be vulnerable and honest and messy with you. you'll meet people who will say "i'm scared i'm too much," or "i don't think i'm enough," and you'll remember we are all tender and afraid at times. and with the right people, you'll work through the tenderness together, instead of waiting to have it all figured out before ever meeting.

love is not something you lose when your heart breaks. this might be hard to believe but love is not something you can lose. it might take years or a lifetime to believe this, and you might forget. you might fight love or fear it. you might chase love or seek it. but until you know that love is not something you rent or borrow it will remain in scarcity. until you stop trying to objectify the untouchable—love will remain untouched. once you know that love is not somewhere because it is everywhere, you will feel its presence completely.

i don't think you understand how much you are loved. they might not say it outright but every grin, every "i'll wait till your uber comes," every bathroom check-in, every, "babe you look so good," is love. it's "how do you take your coffee," and remembering the next time. it's wake-up calls because your alarm didn't work and "you can hang onto the jeans a little longer." it's, "this round is on me," and reading the same book. it's borrowing lighters and teaching each other to knit, 3:00 a.m. phone calls because *i'm drunk and i want to text him.* it's "don't forget your meds," and "i'll go to the pharmacy for you." it's questions to ask at doctor's visits and the same broken heart we'll always help put back together. it's finishing film and endless selfies, it's sharing the pasta and "i have something kind of deep i want to talk about tonight." it's booking flights and meeting parents, it's "my dad can help you with that," and "your hair looks good any color," it's "i'll watch your dog while you're away," and "don't forget to hydrate," and "good morning," "good night," "i miss you." *it's love.*

excitement in love is not the same as chaos. adventure and spontaneity and freedom are not interchangeable with inconsistency and abandonment and distance. a wild, passionate love does not require instability. love, *real love*—tender, safe, and fluid love, love that is built on deep connection, trust, and intimacy, love that honors differences, freedom, and independence, love that seeks to honor and support, not own and merge with—feels like simplicity fueled by zest. love that loves its lovers wants everyone to thrive; so ask yourself if the love you seek feeds or drains you. for while both require tremendous energy, only one produces wildflowers.

you've changed. if by change you mean taken off the masks i wore for you / if by change you mean stopped pretending to be someone else to please the masses / if by change you mean letting go of the world's expectation of me and undressing from the clothes that felt constricting / if by change you mean elaborating less and trusting myself more / if by change you mean expanding into nuance and the place between extremes / if by change you mean staying still because my body is now safely home / if by change you mean *become,* then yeah, *i've changed.*

i feel the tension of the openness:
oh how uncertain we all are.
"it's easier, isn't it, when the choice to
venture into the unknown was yours."
light skies pair with dark liquors.
small glances without hellos remind
me of the loyal bands and i wonder:
who wins this fight?
the heart, or mind?
a tiny light dims beside me and it's time,
it's fine,
or is it,
or was it,
or can it ever be,
to let what is go, and what will be.

OPENING THE MIND

*read this when you doubt yourself.
when your mind plays tricks on
you or old voices creep in. when
you wonder if all that work was
for nothing or if anything will
ever change. read this when life is
testing everything you've worked
for, and you need reminders
of how far you've come.*

despite what it might look like, nobody knows what they're doing. despite what you might hope, there is no road map to being human. despite what it might feel like, you can't do this whole life thing wrong. there is no right way, there is only the way you do it.

it doesn't matter how much therapy you've done. you will still have days when you're convinced you'll never be good enough. that you're too hard to love, or that you're not able to love. you'll get scared and overwhelmed that your heart is too weak—or worse—too broken. that no amount of compassion will give you the courage to trust good things. you'll believe that you're not cut out for love. that you're not somebody who knows how to do it right or that you'll always screw it up. that you'll get too attached or be too distant or want too much or give too little. you'll worry that no matter how much therapy you've done or how much you do you'll always be this way. you'll fear nobody knows how to love anymore, or never did, or that they don't try as much as they used to. you'll fear love is simpler than you're making it and that maybe you're thinking yourself out of all the good parts of love. you'll fear growing older and think you're still too irresponsible to be an adult. you'll wonder how so many people seem to have it figured out while you're making it all up as you go. you'll lose sight of what's important and get sucked into materialism. you'll judge yourself and feel ashamed and often get embarrassed of things you've said or done. but no amount of therapy will strip you of your humanness. you'll learn this well, and learn your health and wellness aren't dependent on perfection, but on acceptance of the mess and uncertainty of it all. because life is messy. and uncertain. and uncomfortable and scary and overwhelming and sometimes it's all too much. you'll remind yourself you're not the only one; that these fears and feelings are part of being human. you'll wish you could swap minds and bodies sometimes. or trade brains for a day just to know for certain you're not alone, or maybe see how others view the world to learn from their perspectives. instead, you'll write. you'll share your fears with lovers and friends. you'll make art and cry in public and ask hard questions. you'll find ways to connect so you can know how not alone you are. you'll find ways to remember that being alive is the wildest ride you'll ever be on. and despite the great unknown and belly full of doubt, you'll hold on with a loose, tender grip, and see it to the very end.

it's not that you don't trust yourself. it's that
there's a *part* of yourself that you don't trust.
find that part. name it. build a relationship with
it: you, the one with softness and compassion,
and them, the one you're learning to trust. repair
the rift as you would with a loved one, and teach
that part of you that trust can be rebuilt.

the part of you that feels unloved or unforgiven / the part of you that feels invisible or empty, like nothing will satiate it as a lover once did / the part of you that wishes for different outcomes or imagines alternate pasts / the part of you that wonders what could have been and fears nothing ever will be: this part of you is overwhelmed and scared because she never learned how to satiate herself, *herself*. this part of you that clings and cries holds on because she never had a safe landing to fall on. this part of you needs you to hold her close, needs your tenderness and safety, needs you to be the one to say, "it will all be ok, you can let go now, i've got you."

if you want to stop doing things that hurt
you, you'll have to start seeing yourself as
someone you don't want to hurt.

did you lose love or did you
just forget love is everywhere?

you'll spend years in therapy learning to love yourself. you'll change your self-talk and show yourself grace and compassion where you once threw criticism. you'll call your mom and ask her if she ever feels panicked in her aloneness or restless by herself. you'll still feel that empty space inside of you. "it feels like a gaping void," you'll say. "like an emptiness that has to be filled, or something terrible might happen." you'll want to know if the scarcity you sometimes feel is just yours, or if it's human. you'll ask yourself whether your feelings or fears or thoughts are disordered or just human nature. you'll come to learn it's likely both/and, where nothing is inherently disordered because the definitions of "normal" or "abnormal" are just a way to make sense of the mystery of being alive. and you won't fully love yourself just yet. despite liking who you are and feeling immensely good about the person you've become, you'll still be self-critical. you'll still be hard on yourself. you'll filter yourself or make yourself small in fear. you'll sit with this realization over coffee one morning and cry. you'll hug yourself and ask, "why am i not enough for me?" you'll rock back and forth with your hands wrapped around your knees and wonder what life might be like if you didn't shrink yourself. what it might be like if you were enough for *you*. how *being enough for you* might soften the not-enoughness you project all around you. so you'll look. you'll look all around you for enough. for good things already. for good things as they are. in gratitude for the good enough, you'll start to notice the love around you. in your friends and family, your dog and small apartment, strangers and flowers and the summer sun. small, good enough, and full of love. maybe it's a temporary victory or small step forward, but you'll hope to keep seeing love everywhere, instead of nowhere to be found. and by loving all that you see around you, you'll learn that loving yourself isn't a final destination but a mode of transportation: loving yourself is how you get on the road, how you get up when you fall, how you roll down the windows to feel the warm air and how you bring passengers along for the ride. you'll start to love yourself the way you pick your fruit and greet your friends. you'll realize all those years in therapy weren't about how to love *yourself*: they were about how to love at all.

your resistance to feeling joy again is your brain trying to protect you from pain; the fear of another loss seems worse than staying sad. but this does not mean you are someone who wants to live this way, and you are deserving of joy and levity right now.

a day of joy or a moment of laughter doesn't erase depression. just like a day of grief or a moment of sorrow doesn't erase contentment. states of being aren't fixed or binary. instead of focusing on changing your feelings, try simply being with them.

you'll know it's time
to ask for help
when the voices in your head
say you don't deserve it.

no matter how many skills you've accrued in therapy, your body and mind will still feel it all. life is unpredictable in the best ways, and in order to find the parts that surprise you with beauty and pleasure, you are bound to be struck by the ones that hurt.

you're going to cry in bathroom stalls and small cafes.
watch sunsets start and end at early hours. a flock
of birds will give you hope, trees turning orange will
give you dancing feet as colder days bring you back
to small cafes. you'll keep warm, home alone, to the
sound of the same flickering voices. phone calls will
tether you to something, someone. a dark night will
feel like endless opportunity; stars will make shapes
that remind you of the infinite universe. mornings
will come and go, come and go, and it will all feel too
repetitive. a tiny blossom on your street corner will
emerge. you'll smell warmer air and remember what
kisses feel like. you're going to cry in bathroom stalls
and small cafes and still, spring will come.

i'm afraid it's all going to fall apart again.
maybe it will.
and if it does,
you don't have to put it back together alone.

what you have to offer doesn't have to be rooted in answers or knowing or finality. what you have to offer can be rooted in hope and courage and vulnerability. be uncertain. be imperfect. be wildly afraid, and show up anyway.

/and then one day/

it dawned on me
nothing is known
and only death is certain
so i might as well embrace this life
while i have it

for anyone with a lifelong confusion about what they're doing / for anyone with anxiety or insecurities / for anyone in transition or a big life change / for anyone with a broken heart or flailing intuition / for anyone battling depression or grief / for anyone starting over or trying again / for anyone questioning their purpose or meaning or why we do all this / for anyone catching up or falling behind / for anyone who feels left out or not part of something bigger / for anyone losing faith or trying to find it / for anyone without direction or changing course / for anyone / *anyone* / anyone: all you can do in every moment is take the next right step, even if it isn't right, even if it's sideways, even if, *even if,* even if. *look up.*

it's in this imperfect home i come to learn
i too, am not symmetrical
that the left side of my face
will never match the right
that i prefer my food 'zero' spicy
and the softness of a woman's forearm
white clothes don't last in my closet
bourbon either
i balance my daily walks with 4 a.m. talks
and i'm not symmetrical
how lovely it is
to grow sideways.

some days you'll walk to the beach. dip your toes in the water. feel the tide swarm around your ankles and remember the version of you that arrived here so long ago. the water will feel the same and the sand will still tickle your skin. the sun will still set like it once did and the ocean spray will smell as salty as before. but the horizon will no longer terrify you. and the place from where you came will no longer entice you. instead, you'll feel a sense of calm as you look out over the water. you'll hug yourself and feel, for the first time, a little more ok with not knowing what comes next.

with age
i come to learn
that all my wounds are temporary,
and the only permanent pain
comes from choosing not to clean them.

maybe healing isn't about a transformation. maybe there are no 'befores' or 'afters.' maybe healing is about realizing we are always right here in the messy middle: where everything is uncertain, nothing is perfect, and anything is possible.

you should be proud of the little things. for making coffee and watering the plants. take pride in your one clean counter or the scratch you gave your pet. chest high for times you cooked a meal and higher when you ate it. be proud of all the little things you did to stay; existence alone is work.

in a lot of ways,
i think that healing
is just aging
with intention.

/it's my birthday/

i used to think i was impervious to aging. like i could somehow stop time from happening. but the truth is, we are always getting older, and our time here is finite. the older i get, the less i worry about my actual age, and the more aware i am that with each passing year, i have one less to be alive. there was a time i welcomed that thought, but i've learned to love my life, so now the thought of dying terrifies me.

i think we all have feelings about death, and none of them are right or wrong; it's the only true certainty in life, and yet the only thing we know nothing about. i think to ease the fear of that inevitable end, it's better to focus on what is known: being alive. so each year on my birthday when i get that little thought that says "oh no, you're getting older," i now gently reply, "and you're still alive today." for now, i know my limited time here is to be treasured, and i don't plan to waste a minute of it.

the older i get, the less interested i am in perfect people. show me your mess. tell me your fears. make mistakes in front of me and let us laugh together. press your forehead to mine and let's giggle through our insecurities because we both know, after all, that scars are simply signs of trying.

maybe they had it wrong
when they said it all works out in the end
maybe it's not about
the end
maybe it's about working it out today
and every day
so that i'm always in a place
where the happy ending
is also the happy beginning.

NAVIGATING FORWARD

read this when you're at the end of things. when you're facing more change. when your heart breaks again or you once again feel stuck. read this when something is over.

a long time ago
i chose to get in the water
knowing how many times
i would have to drown
all so i could find out how it
feels to finally catch a wave.

loss, i've learned, is the nature of life. we are losing today with every ticking second. yesterday is constantly lost, as is tomorrow. i'm dying, and so are you. we are losing everything always. that, i believe, is what grief does best: she arrives in times of great loss to remind us of our impermanence. to shake us and scream, "wake up, this life is fleeting and before you know it, you'll be gone and so will everything you've ever loved." grief is how we remember not to waste the little moments right here, right now.

oh, but *all* things end. this sentence has an ending. each word has a final letter. this doesn't mean another word won't come after the period. nor does it mean more books aren't waiting to be read. resting your head on a pillow at night doesn't mean you won't wake in the morning. and still, you and i both know all things end. i will die. so will you. grief is in everything. *so how do we cope?* how do we allow ourselves to enjoy living, to enjoy the small nourishing moments, to enjoy each other's company while holding the truth that *everything will die*? that endings mean new beginnings, until they don't? perhaps gratitude. holding loosely to what we love. letting go when something is over instead of clinging to something dead. an acknowledgment of the both/and: that this moment is good, and that it too will end.

endings are crushing for some
and liberating for others. either
way, time passes. you choose.

every moment of uncertainty is either a terrifying abyss or a garden to grow. every opportunity to love holds the possibility of loss. grief, and the degree to which we mourn, is only a reflection of our capacity to care. may your hearts stay open, may you feel grief, and may you swim into the unknown or find a garden to grow.

/and then one day/

it was time to leave the home i'd made myself
i outgrew the space, or place
my branches pressed and bent around
the window's edge, it was hard to tell
what was me and what was home
the garden overflowing with flowers outside, inside
my dining table no longer fit
(the friends i'd made)
saying goodbye was bittersweet
for it was in this home, my very
own memories were made
i knew the memories would go with me—tucked
carefully in my pockets like little seeds to plant new
memories with in the next chapter of this little life.
i left the door unlocked for the next tenant, an
invitation to tear it down and start from scratch.
walking towards the beach again
i looked back at the home i'd made
and i was glad to know
i'd taken a chance on myself to begin again

don't be afraid
to begin
again.

i want to believe that life gets to be an adventure. i want to believe that more good things live on the other side of the terrifying. i want to believe that i can always change, i can always learn more, i can always begin again. i feel this more than ever now, sitting at the edge of another year passed: change that has gone and change that's to come. the unexpected people and memories that came from swimming in the deep end and the grief i left behind by making the choice to face forward. it's not easy, facing forward. we don't know what's there—everything ahead is unknown. it's as if we're backstroking through life, only able to see what was left behind but never able to go back. i wonder though, how much scarier it really is to never turn around and look at where we're going. that maybe by facing all that's unknown at least we can choose *some* direction. i don't know. but i want to believe that this place i'm in, this great vast and turbulent water, is the birthing place of more to come: the promise of new horizons, and the reminder that as long as i'm still alive, i can get in the water and swim.

above all else, beyond the material things and milestones, beyond the heartbreak and pain and grief, beyond the accolades and preservation of your legacy beyond the physical end—*above all else*—i hope when you're old or nearing that final end you look back on it all with contentment and sigh, "damn, i had a good time."

what if it's not the end
what if it's simply a new beginning?

when you find yourself at the end of things: breakups or big moves, career changes or graduation, saying goodbye to visitors, airport drop-offs, chucking furniture, donating the jeans you held onto for a body you suffered to live in, the final chapter, the last episode, the death of your favorite character, a plant you couldn't revive, a scarf you knitted all on your own, the band's last set, the songwriter's final album, the plane back home, and the last bite of cake; when you find yourself at the end of things you have two choices: hold on tightly to what you're losing and hope to keep it alive, or be glad it existed at all and let it go. when you find yourself at the end of things you'll remember the sand between your toes and how you weren't ready to swim. when you find yourself at the end of things you'll remember how you swam across vast waters and saw new places. when you find yourself at the end of things you'll remember the home you built and the garden you grew from scratch. you'll remember the hands you held and lovers you embraced. you'll remember the fear you felt and how you loved yourself anyway. you'll remember the version of you that didn't believe this life was worth it, and the version of you today that knows it is. you'll see that you've become someone you dreamed might exist, and this version of you knows that endings deserve thoughtful goodbyes. you'll know to stand at the water's edge and thank the sand beneath your feet for leading you this far. you'll hold yourself tenderly and smile, because you'll know how much life there is left to live, and how the only reason you can see this now is because you had the courage to look up.

/the beginning/

Cronin was clearly surprised at that, and he paused to stare out across London for a moment. "It's fitting in a way," he said. "That despite never becoming king, you are elder of the London coven—the leader of England's vampires, if you will. You were born for it. Not the crown you should have worn, perhaps, but a great leader nonetheless."

"What are you saying, Cronin?" Kennard asked. "Do you think my decision to step down is a foolish one?"

"No," he answered with a smile. "I think you need to do what makes you happy. Though I do think your coven will miss you. I think England will be at a loss without you on the council."

Kennard took a deep breath and snuggled into Stas' side some more. "Well, I haven't decided yet. Not completely. Though I have promoted Stephanie to be General Manager of my company. She's been overseeing everything in my absence anyway, and she's more than capable. Then I'm not so obligated to stay, and Stas and I are free to spend time wherever we choose."

"Oh," Cronin said, making a face. "Uh, Kennard. Remember that time we were in Westminster Abbey and I sat in the coronation chair and Alec and I joked about stealing it." He grimaced. "I apologize for that. We made a mockery of your family history, of the chair your father was crowned in, and over the centuries, for all the times I've mocked England—"

Kennard raised his hand, palm forward. "Stop, Cronin. There is no need to apologize. Actually, I'll be very disappointed if you stop making a mockery of the English royal family. I enjoy our little spats over who is better." Kennard sniffed. "Which we all know the answer to. England is clearly superior in every way."

Cronin laughed at that, and Stas gave Kennard a

squeeze. "I have my very own prince," Stas said with a smile. "Though I ask him if he is king, then would I be queen?"

Kennard snorted. "Which is ridiculous, right? Because out of the two of us, I think we all know who the flaming queen is."

Alec and Cronin laughed, and Kennard sighed contentedly.

Yes, contentedly. He'd never been more content.

He had his mate, his friends, and he now had the freedom to choose where to spend his time, and where he could enjoy living. Something he hadn't truly ever done before.

"Oh, that does remind me," Cronin said. "Speaking of the coronation chair. It supposedly once held the Stone of Destiny. Put there by King Edward I, who would be your great, great, great—"

"No," Kennard said loudly. "No. No more stones of destiny, no more philosopher's stone, no more Cintamani stone, or the Coyolxauhqui stone, no more *blood from a stone, stone from a blood*," he imitated Jorge's voice. "I'm kind of done with the whole stone thing. For a while, at least."

Alec laughed. "But if something raises its ugly head, you have to help us. It's not the complete Scooby-Doo Gang without you. Without both of you."

Kennard sighed dramatically. "Well, that's true. Every crime-fighting team does require the handsome Russian and his dashing Englishman mate. It does counterweight the"— he scrunched his nose up at Cronin—"Scottish riffraff."

They all laughed, then were quiet for a moment, until Alec snorted and Kennard realized that Stas and Alec were having a silent conversation.

"Do Cronin and I even want to know what you two are saying?" Kennard asked.

Alec grinned. "I was just discussing with Stas what he decided."

Kennard looked up at Stas. "About keeping his ability to read minds?"

"So, have you made a decision?" Cronin asked Stas.

Stas gave a hard nod. "Yes. I have."

Kennard sat up and threaded his fingers with Stas' once more. His hand looked so small in Stas' huge hand, and it made him smile.

"I can keep the block in your mind if you want," Alec said.

Stas blushed but shook his head. "Thank you, but no. I like hearing my Kennard's mind." He shrugged one shoulder. "But also to protect him. I will keep my mind reading."

Kennard and Stas had discussed this at length in the four days since they'd returned from their trip to Atlantis. Kennard didn't want Stas to do something for his sake. If he wanted to keep his mind-reading ability, then he should do it for the right reasons. How incredible it made their lovemaking aside, if it was going to drive Stas crazy being in London or New York or Tokyo, then Kennard would rather Stas didn't keep it.

But Stas was adamant.

"We make compromise," Stas said with a smile.

Kennard chuckled. "We did. Stas wants to stay in London. He loves the apartment, loves the nightlife, and he even let me fit out half my wardrobe with new clothes for him."

Cronin laughed. "I like the new look," he said. It was true. Stas filled out designer clothes just as well as his lumberjack outfits.

"Thanks," Stas said. "Different from taking clothes from dinner dates."

That made Kennard laugh. "Must have limited your selection, my love."

"No," Stas said with a grin. "Men in Russian wilds are big like me."

Kennard hummed, and he couldn't help the pang of longing he felt.

"Kennard?" Alec said. "Something you'd like to share?"

"Well, yes," he said, giving Stas a coy smile. "We compromised on a few things. We will keep this apartment for Stas, and I want to build a house in the forest of Northern Russia. When the voices get too much and Stas needs a break, we'll have the blissful peace and quiet of the Far Northern wilds."

Cronin laughed at that. "Who would have thought it? You, being at home in the isolated forests of any country that is not England."

"Oh shut up," Kennard said, though he smiled. "But you're right. I loved being at Stas' cabin. I love how rustic it is and how intimate it is. It feels like a home."

"It does," Alec agreed. "Our cottage in Scotland is amazing."

"You've just finished the renovations, yes?" Kennard asked.

Alec gave a nod. "Yes. It's utterly perfect. Sammy the cat is very happy there."

"That reminds me," Kennard said. "How are Kole and Eleanor?"

"Dad's great. Eleanor keeps him in line," Alec said. "They've been staying in Japan at Eiji's house. He loves it there."

"I'm glad. Give them both my best wishes."

"I will." Then Alec frowned at Kennard. "What was that? That visual didn't make much sense."

Kennard sighed wistfully. "I just wish we could pick the cabin up from where it is and drop it about a hundred miles north of where it is," he replied.

Alec made a face. "I've never tried to leap a house before... I could try? I've done a car, but not a house."

Kennard laughed. "Well, we haven't bought the land yet."

"And he wants basement. And this fancy glass," Stas added, waving at the wall of window. "And shower with jets. And cinema room. And library."

Kennard grinned. "Just a few little luxuries."

Cronin laughed. "There's the Kennard I know."

Alec grinned too. "Well, let me know when you settle on the land or location or whatever. If I can't leap an entire house, I might be able to replicate one." He shrugged. "Can't hurt to try."

"You didn't try and replicate anything in your cottage?" Kennard asked. "Not even once?"

"No," Alec said. "Though the tradesmen were impressed with how fast I could get things delivered. Shipments of tiles, flooring, fixtures from anywhere around the world, would just appear overnight." He winked.

Kennard grinned and Stas pulled him in for a kiss. "You have bestest friends." Then Stas turned to Alec. "But you can keep weirdness and statues that move and basilisks."

Alec laughed. "Oh come on, guys. Weird is fun every now and then."

"Do me a favor, Alec, darling," Kennard said. "Give us a hundred years before we need to save the world again, okay?"

"I'll see what I can do. The pits below the Hagia Sophia

church in Istanbul aren't supposed to reopen for another two hundred years or so."

Two hundred years? Kennard sighed happily. He snuggled back into Stas' side and smiled when Stas' huge arm settled over his shoulder. "I can live with that."

THE END

ABOUT THE AUTHOR

N.R. Walker is an Australian author, who loves her genre of gay romance. She loves writing and spends far too much time doing it, but wouldn't have it any other way.

She is many things: a mother, a wife, a sister, a writer. She has pretty, pretty boys who live in her head, who don't let her sleep at night unless she gives them life with words.

She likes it when they do dirty, dirty things... but likes it even more when they fall in love.

She used to think having people in her head talking to her was weird, until one day she happened across other writers who told her it was normal.

She's been writing ever since...

LOOK UP.

/a thank you/

i want to thank my dear friends who sat with me in my doubt and helped me navigate all the unknowns of writing this book. a special thank you to sabine cafe (where most of this book was written) for the endless coffee and encouragement. and the deepest gratitude for my family—who has supported me in every challenging season of my life—for always believing i'd one day find my horizon.

RACHEL HAVEKOST is a bestselling author with roots in psychology, theater, and education. After over a decade of battling an eating disorder, suicidal depression, and anxiety, she started writing about her therapeutic discoveries in hopes of helping one person feel less alone. After getting divorced during the pandemic, she shared stories of living boldly and choosing to live on her own terms. Now, her work centers around reminding people that life is worth living, even amidst great uncertainty, even when we're terrified, and especially when we're unsure what lies on the horizon.

Instagram @rachel_havekost
TikTok @rachelhavekost
Threads @rachel_havekost
www.rachelhavekost.com
rachelhavekost.substack.com

ALSO BY N.R. WALKER

Red Dirt Heart 3

Red Dirt Heart 4

The Weight Of It All

Switched

Point of No Return

Breaking Point

Starting Point

Spencer Cohen Book One

Spencer Cohen Book Two

Spencer Cohen Book Three

Yanni's Story

On Davis Row

Evolved

Free Reads:

Sixty Five Hours

Learning to Feel

His Grandfather's Watch (And The Story of Billy and Hale)

The Twelfth of Never (Blind Faith 3.5)

Twelve Days of Christmas (Sixty Five Hours Christmas)

Best of Both Worlds

Translated Titles:

Fiducia Cieca (Italian translation of Blind Faith)

MORE FROM
THOUGHT CATALOG BOOKS

The Art Of Who We Are
Robert W. Dean

The Gods We Made
Blake Auden

And Yet, Here You Are
Eileen Lamb

It Is All Equally Fragile
Alison Malee

The Words We Left Behind
Callie Byrnes

Moments To Hold Close
Molly Burford

Face Yourself. Look Within.
Adrian Michael

Eyes On The Road
Michell C. Clark

THOUGHT
CATALOG
Books

THOUGHTCATALOG.COM